HOW TO MASTER YOUR MIND

[MEET RAO]

Master Your Mind: A Practical Guide to Unlocking Your Full Potential

Introduction:

Welcome to Master Your Mind, a practical guide to unlocking your full potential. In this book, we will explore the power of the mind and how to harness it for success in all areas of your life. Our minds are incredibly powerful tools, but many of us do not fully understand how to use them to their fullest potential. By the end of this book, you will have the knowledge and skills necessary to master your mind and achieve your goals.

Chapter 1: Understanding the Mind-Body Connection

In this chapter, we will explore the connection between the mind and the body. We will discuss the different parts of the brain and their functions, as well as the role of the nervous system in controlling our thoughts and emotions. We will also explore the mind-body connection and how our thoughts and emotions can impact our physical health.

Chapter 2: The Power of Positive Thinking

In this chapter, we will discuss the power of positive thinking and how it can impact our lives. We will explore the concept of the law of attraction and how to use positive affirmations to reprogram our minds for success. We will also discuss the importance of visualization and how to use it to achieve your goals.

Chapter 3: Overcoming Limiting Beliefs1

In this chapter, we will explore the concept of limiting beliefs and how they can hold us back from achieving our full potential. We will discuss common limiting beliefs and how to overcome them through techniques such as reframing and cognitive restructuring.

Chapter 4: Developing a Growth Mindset

In this chapter, we will explore the concept of a growth mindset and how it can help us achieve our goals. We will discuss the difference between a growth mindset and a fixed mindset, and how to develop a growth mindset through techniques such as embracing challenges, learning from failure, and seeking out feedback.

Chapter 5: Mindfulness and Meditation

In this chapter, we will explore the concepts of mindfulness and meditation and their benefits for the mind and body. We will discuss different mindfulness techniques such as breathwork and body scanning, as well as different meditation practices such as guided meditation and mantra meditation.

Chapter 6: Goal Setting and Action Planning

In this chapter, we will discuss the importance of goal setting and action planning for achieving our goals. We will explore different goal-setting frameworks such as SMART goals, and how to break down larger goals into smaller, actionable steps. We will also discuss the importance of accountability and how to hold yourself accountable for your goals.

Chapter 7: The Role of Habits in Mind Mastery

In this chapter, we will explore the role of habits in mastering the mind. We will discuss the different types of habits and how to develop positive habits through techniques such as habit stacking and habit tracking. We will also discuss how to break negative habits and replace them with positive ones.

Chapter 8: Managing Stress and Anxiety

In this chapter, we will explore techniques for managing stress and anxiety, which can impact our mental and physical health. We will discuss the different types of stress and anxiety, and how to recognize and manage them through techniques such as mindfulness, relaxation techniques, and cognitive behavioral therapy.

Chapter 9: The Importance of Self-Care

In this chapter, we will explore the concept of self-care and its importance for mental and physical health. We will discuss different self-care techniques such as exercise, healthy eating, and time management, and how to prioritize self-care in your daily routine.

Chapter 10: Putting it all Together

In this final chapter, we will bring together all of the concepts and techniques discussed in this book and provide a framework for mastering your mind. We will discuss the importance of consistent practice and ongoing learning, and how to continue to grow and develop your

Chapter 11: Cultivating Positive Self Talk

The way we talk to ourselves has a profound impact on our mood, behavior, and overall well-being. Negative self-talk, such as "I'm not good enough" or "I'll never be able to do this," can erode our self-confidence and limit our potential. In contrast, positive self-talk can boost our self-esteem, increase our motivation, and improve our mental health.

Chapter 1: Understanding the Mind-Body Connection

The mind-body connection is the relationship between a person's thoughts, emotions, and physical health. It is the idea that the mind and body are not separate entities, but rather, they are interconnected and affect each other in a multitude of ways.

There are several ways to understand the mind-body connection, including:

Psychological factors: Psychological factors, such as stress, anxiety, and depression, can have a significant impact on a person's physical health. When a person experiences chronic stress or anxiety, their body may produce more cortisol, a hormone associated with the body's stress response, which can lead to a variety of physical health problems over time.

Biological factors: Biological factors, such as genetics and hormones, can also play a role in the mind-body connection. For example, certain genetic mutations can increase a person's risk for developing certain mental health disorders, which can in turn affect their physical health. Similarly, hormonal imbalances can cause mood swings, fatigue, and other physical symptoms.

Lifestyle factors: Lifestyle factors, such as diet, exercise, and sleep, can also impact the mind-body connection. Eating a healthy diet and getting enough exercise can improve mood and reduce stress, which can in turn improve physical health. Conversely, a lack of sleep or unhealthy eating habits can have negative effects on both mental and physical health.

Understanding the mind-body connection can have significant implications for healthcare. Many healthcare providers now recognize the importance of addressing both the mental and physical health of their patients in order to provide comprehensive care. This can involve treating mental health disorders alongside physical health problems, or incorporating stress-reduction techniques into a patient's treatment plan.

Overall, the mind-body connection is a complex and multifaceted concept that requires a holistic approach to understand and address. By recognizing the interplay between mental and physical health, individuals and healthcare providers can work towards promoting optimal health and wellbeing.

The link between our minds and bodies holds a well of potential when it came to radical healing — even mainstream medicine accepts that our stress levels and thought patterns, for example, can impact our physical health."

窗体顶端

Chapter 2: The Power of Positive Thinking

The power of positive thinking is a concept that has been around for centuries and is based on the belief that having a positive attitude can lead to positive outcomes in life. The idea is that when we focus on positive thoughts, we attract positive experiences and opportunities into our lives, while negative thinking can attract negative experiences.

Research has shown that the power of positive thinking can have significant effects on our mental and physical health, relationships, and overall wellbeing. Here are some ways that positive thinking can impact our lives:

Mental health: Positive thinking can help to reduce stress, anxiety, and depression. When we focus on positive thoughts, we are less likely to dwell on negative experiences or thoughts that can lead to feelings of anxiety or sadness.

Physical health: Studies have shown that positive thinking can lead to better physical health outcomes, including lower blood pressure, improved immune function, and better cardiovascular health.

Relationships: Positive thinking can improve relationships with others by creating a more optimistic and open mindset. When we approach relationships with positivity, we are more likely to attract positive people and experiences into our lives.

Success: The power of positive thinking has also been linked to success in personal and professional goals. When we believe in ourselves and our abilities, we are more likely to take risks, persist through challenges, and achieve our goals.

So how can we cultivate positive thinking in our lives? Here are some strategies:

Practice gratitude: Focusing on the things we are grateful for can shift our mindset from negative to positive. Make a habit of writing down three things you are grateful for each day.

Reframe negative thoughts: When negative thoughts arise, try to reframe them in a more positive light. For example, if you receive negative feedback at work, try to see it as an opportunity for growth and improvement.

Surround yourself with positivity: Surrounding yourself with positive people and experiences can help to reinforce a positive mindset. Seek out uplifting activities and spend time with people who uplift and inspire you.

Visualize success: Visualization is a powerful tool for creating positive outcomes. Spend time each day visualizing yourself achieving your goals and experiencing success.

In conclusion, the power of positive thinking is a real and impactful concept that can lead to significant improvements in our lives. By cultivating positivity through gratitude, reframing negative thoughts, surrounding ourselves with positivity, and visualizing success, we can create a more optimistic and fulfilling life.

窗体顶端

窗体底端

THINK IT,
WANT IT,
GET IT

Chapter 3 : Overcoming Limiting Beliefs

The beliefs that we hold in our mind have a powerful influence on our behavior and emotions. They shape our perception of reality and determine how we respond to the world around us. However, sometimes our beliefs can be limiting or inaccurate, causing us to feel anxious, depressed, or stuck in our lives. In order to live a fulfilling and happy life, it is essential to learn how to overcome these beliefs.

The first step in overcoming beliefs of the mind is to become aware of them. Often, our beliefs operate on a subconscious level, so we may not even realize that we hold certain beliefs. Taking the time to reflect on our thoughts and emotions can help us identify the beliefs that are limiting us.

Once we have identified our beliefs, it is important to challenge them. We should ask ourselves if they are true, helpful, or limiting in any way. We should also consider alternative perspectives and seek out new information that contradicts our beliefs.

For example, if we believe that we are not good enough to pursue our dreams, we can challenge this belief by looking for evidence that supports the opposite view. We can read stories of people who have overcome similar challenges or seek the advice of a mentor who has experience in our field.

In addition to challenging our beliefs, it is important to practice mindfulness. Mindfulness can help us become more aware of our thoughts and feelings, without getting caught up in them. This can help us recognize when our beliefs are causing us distress and allow us to choose a more helpful thought.

We can also take action to overcome our limiting beliefs. Sometimes, the best way to overcome a fear or limiting belief is to face it head-on. For example, if we are afraid of public speaking, we can take a public speaking class or seek out opportunities to speak in front of others.

Finally, it is important to be patient with ourselves as we work to overcome our beliefs of the mind. Changing our beliefs is a process that takes time and effort. We may make mistakes along the way, but it is important to stay committed to our goal of living a fulfilling and happy life.

In conclusion, overcoming beliefs of the mind is an important step in achieving happiness and fulfillment. By becoming aware of our beliefs, challenging them, practicing mindfulness, taking action, and being patient, we can learn to overcome our limiting beliefs and live the life we desire.

Overcoming beliefs of the mind can be a challenging task, but it is not impossible. Here are some strategies that can help:

Recognize your beliefs: The first step is to identify your beliefs. Ask yourself what you believe about a particular situation, person, or thing. Write them down, and then try to analyze them.

Challenge your beliefs: Once you have identified your beliefs, it is important to question them. Ask yourself if they are true, if they are helpful, or if they are limiting you in any way. Try to see the situation from a different perspective and consider alternative explanations.

Gather new information: Seek out new information that challenges your beliefs. Read books, talk to people who have different opinions, or seek out experiences that will challenge your current beliefs.

Practice mindfulness: Mindfulness can help you become more aware of your thoughts and feelings. By practicing mindfulness, you can learn to observe your thoughts without getting caught up in them. This can help you recognize when your beliefs are causing you distress.

Take action: Sometimes, the best way to overcome beliefs of the mind is to take action. If you are afraid of public speaking, for example, the best way to overcome that fear may be to take a public speaking class.

Remember that changing your beliefs is a process that takes time and effort. Be patient with yourself and be willing to make mistakes along the way. With practice, you can learn to overcome limiting beliefs and live a more fulfilling life.

Chapter 4 : Developing a Growth Mindset

In recent years, the idea of a growth mindset has become increasingly popular as a way to achieve personal and professional growth. A growth mindset is the belief that one's abilities and intelligence can be developed through hard work, dedication, and learning. In contrast, a fixed mindset is the belief that abilities and intelligence are predetermined and cannot be changed.

Developing a growth mindset is essential for success in all aspects of life. Here are some steps you can take to cultivate a growth mindset:

Embrace challenges

One of the most important things you can do to develop a growth mindset is to embrace challenges. Instead of avoiding difficult tasks, view them as opportunities for growth and learning. When you encounter a challenge, try to approach it with an open mind and a willingness to learn.

Learn from failure

Failure is an inevitable part of life, but it doesn't have to be a negative experience. Instead of viewing failure as a reflection of your abilities, see it as an opportunity to learn and grow. Take the time to reflect on what went wrong and what you can do differently next time.

Cultivate a love of learning

People with a growth mindset are always looking for ways to learn and improve. You can cultivate a love of learning by seeking out new experiences, reading books, attending workshops or classes, and engaging in hobbies that challenge you.

Adopt a positive attitude

A positive attitude can go a long way in developing a growth mindset. Instead of focusing on your limitations and shortcomings, try to focus on your strengths and the possibilities that lie ahead. Surround yourself with positive people who support and encourage you.

Set goals

Setting goals is an important part of developing a growth mindset. When you set goals, you are creating a roadmap for your personal and professional growth. Make sure your goals are specific, measurable, and achievable, and don't be afraid to revise them as you learn and grow.

Practice perseverance

Perseverance is key to developing a growth mindset. When faced with obstacles, don't give up. Instead, keep pushing forward and trying new strategies until you achieve your goals.

In conclusion, developing a growth mindset is essential for personal and professional growth. By embracing challenges, learning from failure, cultivating a love of learning, adopting a positive attitude, setting goals, and practicing perseverance, you can develop a growth mindset that will serve you well throughout your life.

Chapter 5 : Mindfulness and Meditation

In today's fast-paced world, it's becoming increasingly challenging to stay focused and centered. With so many distractions and responsibilities, it's easy to feel overwhelmed, stressed, and anxious. Fortunately, mindfulness and meditation are powerful tools that can help you cultivate inner peace, reduce stress, and improve your overall well-being. In this article, we will explore the benefits of mindfulness and meditation and how to get started with a regular practice.

What is mindfulness?

Mindfulness is the practice of being fully present and engaged in the moment, without judgment or distraction. It involves paying attention to your thoughts, feelings, and sensations in the present moment, and accepting them without trying to change or control them.

Mindfulness can help you become more aware of your thoughts and emotions, which can improve your ability to regulate them. It can also help you cultivate a greater sense of compassion and empathy towards yourself and others.

What is meditation?

Meditation is a practice that involves training your mind to focus on a particular object, such as your breath or a mantra, in order to achieve a state of calm and relaxation. Meditation has been practiced for thousands of years and is often associated with spiritual and religious practices.

However, meditation can also be a secular practice and is increasingly being used in healthcare settings to improve mental health and well-being. There are many different types of meditation, including mindfulness meditation, loving-kindness meditation, and transcendental meditation.

Benefits of mindfulness and meditation

Research has shown that regular mindfulness and meditation practice can have numerous benefits, including:

Reduced stress and anxiety

Mindfulness and meditation can help reduce stress and anxiety by promoting relaxation and helping you develop a greater sense of inner calm and peace.

Improved focus and concentration

Regular mindfulness and meditation practice can help improve your ability to focus and concentrate, which can improve your productivity and effectiveness.

Increased self-awareness

Mindfulness and meditation can help you become more aware of your thoughts and emotions, which can help you better understand yourself and your behaviors.

Greater compassion and empathy

Mindfulness and meditation can help you cultivate a greater sense of compassion and empathy towards yourself and others, which can improve your relationships and overall well-being.

Getting started with mindfulness and meditation

If you're interested in getting started with mindfulness and meditation, here are some tips to help you establish a regular practice:

Start small

It's important to start small and gradually build up your practice. Start with just a few minutes of mindfulness or meditation each day and gradually increase the time as you become more comfortable.

Find a quiet, comfortable space

Find a quiet, comfortable space where you can sit or lie down without being disturbed. You may also want to use cushions or props to help you sit comfortably.

Choose a technique that works for you

There are many different techniques and styles of mindfulness and meditation, so choose one that resonates with you. You may want to try different techniques until you find one that feels comfortable and effective for you.

Practice regularly

Regular practice is essential for experiencing the benefits of mindfulness and meditation. Try to practice every day, even if it's just for a few minutes.

In conclusion, mindfulness and meditation are powerful tools that can help you cultivate inner peace, reduce stress, and improve your overall well-being. By starting small, finding a quiet space, choosing a technique that works for you, and practicing regularly, you can establish a regular mindfulness and meditation practice that will serve you well for years to come.

Chapter 6:Goal Setting and Action Planning

Setting goals and creating an action plan to achieve them is an essential part of personal and professional growth. Whether you're looking to advance in your career, improve your health, or develop a new skill, having a clear set of goals and a plan to achieve them is crucial to your success. In this article, we'll explore the benefits of goal setting and action planning, as well as strategies for setting effective goals and creating actionable plans.

Why is goal setting important?

Goal setting is important for several reasons:

Provides direction and focus: Setting goals helps you clarify what you want to achieve and gives you direction and focus to work towards it.

Increases motivation: Having clear goals and a plan to achieve them can increase your motivation and commitment to the task at hand.

Enhances performance: Setting specific, measurable, and challenging goals can help you achieve higher levels of performance.

Boosts self-confidence: Achieving your goals can give you a sense of accomplishment and boost your self-confidence.

Creating an Action Plan

Once you have set your goals, it's essential to create an action plan that outlines the steps you will take to achieve them. An action plan is a detailed roadmap that breaks down your goals into smaller, actionable steps. Here are some tips for creating an effective action plan:

Break down your goals: Break your goals down into smaller, manageable tasks. This will make them less overwhelming and easier to tackle.

Set deadlines: Assign deadlines to each task to keep yourself accountable and on track.

Identify resources: Identify the resources you need to accomplish your tasks, such as time, money, or equipment.

Prioritize: Prioritize your tasks based on their importance and urgency.

Review and adjust: Review your action plan regularly and make adjustments as necessary.

Setting Effective Goals

To set effective goals, you need to make sure they are specific, measurable, achievable, relevant, and time-bound (SMART). Here's what that means:

Specific: Your goals should be clear and specific, with a defined outcome.

Measurable: Your goals should have specific metrics or criteria for success so that you can track progress.

Achievable: Your goals should be challenging but achievable, considering your resources and abilities.

Relevant: Your goals should be relevant to your overall objectives and aligned with your values.

Time-bound: Your goals should have a specific timeframe completion, so for you can stay focused and track progress.

Tips for Achieving Your Goals

Here are some tips to help you achieve your goals:

Stay motivated: Keep yourself motivated by reminding yourself of why you set the goal and the benefits it will bring.

Take action: Take action every day, no matter how small, to move closer to your goal.

Celebrate your achievements: Celebrate your achievements along the way to keep yourself motivated.

Stay flexible: Be open to adjusting your action plan if necessary, and don't be afraid to try new strategies.

Seek support: Seek support from friends, family, or a coach to help keep you accountable and motivated.

In conclusion, setting goals and creating an action plan is essential to personal and professional growth. By following the SMART criteria for setting goals, breaking them down into smaller, manageable tasks, and creating an actionable plan, you can achieve your objectives and improve your overall well-being. Remember to stay motivated, take action every day, celebrate your achievements, stay flexible, and seek support when needed. With determination and a solid plan, you can achieve your goals and reach your full potential.

Chapter 7: The Role of Habits in Mind Mastery

Habits play a crucial role in mind mastery as they provide a framework for behavior and actions. The mind is a complex entity that requires discipline and focus to function optimally. The habits we cultivate have a profound impact on our thought patterns, emotions, and behavior. Developing positive habits is therefore an essential aspect of achieving mind mastery.

Habits are automatic patterns of behavior that are repeated regularly. They can be beneficial or harmful, depending on their nature. Positive habits contribute to a healthy and productive lifestyle, while negative habits can hinder progress and lead to self-destructive behavior.

To achieve mind mastery, it is important to identify and cultivate positive habits. These habits can include meditation, exercise, healthy eating, reading, and self-reflection. By incorporating these habits into our daily routine, we create a sense of structure and purpose that helps us to stay focused and motivated.

Meditation is a particularly powerful habit for mind mastery as it helps to cultivate mindfulness and awareness. By practicing meditation regularly, we learn to observe our thoughts and emotions without judgment, which can help us to develop greater emotional intelligence and resilience.

Exercise is another essential habit for mind mastery as it not only improves physical health but also promotes mental clarity and reduces stress. Regular exercise has been shown to improve mood and cognitive function, making it an important habit for anyone looking to achieve mind mastery.

Healthy eating is also crucial for mind mastery, as the food we consume can have a significant impact on our mood and energy levels. A diet rich in fruits, vegetables, and whole grains can provide the nutrients our bodies need to function optimally, while also improving our mental health.

Reading is another important habit for mind mastery as it helps to expand our knowledge and understanding of the world around us. By reading regularly, we expose ourselves to new ideas and perspectives, which can help us to develop a more open-minded and empathetic outlook.

Finally, self-reflection is an essential habit for mind mastery as it allows us to examine our thoughts and behavior patterns in a non-judgmental way. By reflecting on our experiences, we can gain insights into our strengths and weaknesses, and develop greater self-awareness and emotional intelligence.

In conclusion, habits play a vital role in mind mastery as they provide a framework for behavior and actions. By cultivating positive habits such as meditation, exercise, healthy eating, reading, and self-reflection, we can create a sense of structure and purpose in our lives, and develop the discipline and focus necessary to achieve greater mental clarity and emotional resilience.

Chapter 8 : Managing Stress and Anxiety

Stress and anxiety are common experiences that can arise due to a variety of factors, including work, relationships, finances, health issues, and everyday situations such as traffic or crowded spaces. These feelings are a normal part of life, but when they become chronic and overwhelming, they can interfere with daily activities and negatively impact mental and physical health. Here are some strategies that can help manage stress and anxiety:

Exercise Exercise is a proven way to reduce stress and anxiety. It can increase the production of endorphins, which are natural mood-boosters. Exercise can also help to reduce muscle tension, improve sleep quality, and promote relaxation. Aim for at least 30 minutes of physical activity each day, such as walking, jogging, cycling, or swimming.

Mindfulness Meditation Mindfulness meditation is a practice that involves paying attention to the present moment without judgment. By focusing on the present moment, we can become aware of our thoughts and feelings and learn to accept them without getting caught up in them. This can help to reduce stress and anxiety and promote a sense of calm. Try setting aside 10-15 minutes each day for mindfulness meditation.

Deep Breathing Deep breathing is a simple technique that can be done anywhere and anytime to help manage stress and anxiety. By taking slow, deep breaths, we can activate the parasympathetic nervous system, which helps to calm the body and reduce stress. To practice deep breathing, sit or lie down in a quiet place, close your eyes, and inhale deeply through your nose, then exhale slowly through your mouth.

Time Management Poor time management can contribute to stress and anxiety. By setting priorities and planning ahead, we can reduce the feeling of being overwhelmed and create a sense of control. Make a to-do list and prioritize tasks, delegate responsibilities when possible, and schedule breaks throughout the day.

Social Support Social support can be an effective way to manage stress and anxiety. Talking to friends or family members, joining a support group, or seeking professional help can provide a sense of connection and support during difficult times. Reach out to loved ones and consider seeking therapy or counseling if necessary.

Healthy Lifestyle Eating a healthy diet, getting enough sleep, and avoiding drugs and alcohol can all contribute to reducing stress and anxiety. Aim for a balanced diet that includes plenty of fruits, vegetables, and whole grains, and avoid foods high in sugar and caffeine. Make sleep a priority and aim for 7-8 hours of sleep each night. Avoid using drugs and alcohol to cope with stress and anxiety, as this can lead to more problems in the long run.

Cognitive-Behavioral Therapy Cognitive-behavioral therapy is a type of therapy that focuses on changing negative thought patterns and behaviors. It can be effective in treating anxiety and stress-related disorders. If stress and anxiety are impacting your daily life, consider seeking professional help from a therapist or counselor.

In conclusion, managing stress and anxiety requires a multifaceted approach that includes healthy lifestyle habits, stress-reducing techniques, and seeking professional help if necessary. By incorporating these strategies into our daily routine, we can learn to manage stress and anxiety and promote overall mental and physical health. Remember, it is essential to take care of yourself both physically and emotionally to lead a happy and healthy life.

Chapter 9 : The Importance of Self Care

Self-care is the act of taking care of oneself both physically and emotionally. It involves intentionally engaging in activities that promote well-being and reduce stress. The importance of self-care cannot be overstated, as it is crucial for maintaining good mental and physical health. Here are some key reasons why self-care is essential:

Improved Mental Health: Practicing self-care helps to reduce stress, anxiety, and depression. It can improve our mood, increase our self-esteem, and boost our overall sense of well-being.

Better Physical Health: Self-care practices such as exercise, healthy eating, and getting enough sleep can improve our physical health. By taking care of our bodies, we reduce the risk of chronic diseases and maintain a better quality of life.

Increased Productivity: Taking time to practice self-care can actually increase our productivity. When we take care of ourselves, we have more energy and focus, which helps us to be more efficient and effective in our work.

Improved Relationships: When we take care of ourselves, we are better equipped to handle the challenges of relationships. We are more patient, understanding, and compassionate, which can help to improve our relationships with others.

Reduced Burnout: Self-care can help to prevent burnout, a state of physical, emotional, and mental exhaustion caused by prolonged stress. When we prioritize self-care, we can avoid getting to the point of burnout, which can have serious consequences for our health and well-being.

In conclusion, self-care is essential for maintaining good mental and physical health. By engaging in activities that promote well-being and reduce stress, we can improve our mood, increase our productivity, and build stronger relationships. Remember to prioritize self-care in your daily life and make it a priority. By taking care of yourself, you can lead a happier, healthier, and more fulfilling life.

Self-care also involves setting boundaries and saying "no" to things that do not serve our best interests. It is important to recognize that taking care of oneself is not a luxury or a selfish act, but rather a fundamental aspect of maintaining a healthy and fulfilling life.

Chapter 10 : Putting it all Together

Putting it all together involves taking the various steps and practices of self-improvement and integrating them into your daily life. By doing so, you can create a sustainable and holistic approach to personal growth and development. Here are some key steps to help you put it all together:

Set Goals: Start by identifying specific goals that you want to achieve. Whether it's improving your mental health, building stronger relationships, or pursuing a new career, having a clear sense of what you want to achieve will help you stay motivated and focused.

Develop a Plan: Once you have identified your goals, develop a plan for achieving them. This may involve breaking down your goals into smaller, more manageable tasks, and setting deadlines for each step.

Practice Mindful Awareness: Practice mindfulness meditation or other techniques that help you to observe your thoughts and emotions without judgment. This will help you to develop a greater sense of self-awareness and make more intentional choices.

Challenge Negative Thoughts: Identify negative thought patterns and challenge them with positive affirmations or by reframing them in a more positive light. This will help you to develop a more positive and resilient mindset.

Practice Self-Care: Develop positive habits that support your mental and physical well-being, such as regular exercise, healthy eating, and getting enough sleep. Prioritizing self-care will help you to build resilience and better cope with stress.

Connect with Others: Build supportive relationships with friends, family, or a therapist. Share your thoughts and feelings with others and seek support when needed. Building a support system will help you to stay motivated and accountable.

Evaluate and Adjust: Regularly evaluate your progress and adjust your plan as needed. Celebrate your successes and learn from your mistakes.

By following these steps, you can create a personalized approach to personal growth and development that integrates mindfulness, positive thinking, self-care, and social support. Remember that personal growth is a lifelong journey and that it takes consistent effort and practice. With time and dedication, you can achieve your goals and live a more fulfilling life.

"Putting it all together is the key to success in any area of life. By combining intention with action, mindfulness with positive thinking, and self-care with social support, we can create a powerful and holistic approach to personal growth and development."

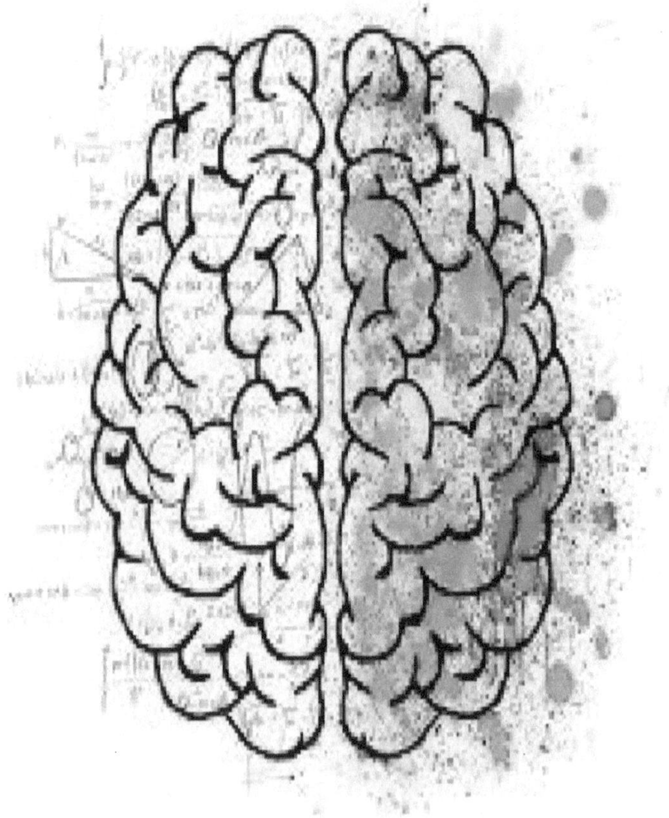

Chapter 11 : Cultivating Positive Self Talk

The way we talk to ourselves has a profound impact on our mood, behavior, and overall well-being. Negative self-talk, such as "I'm not good enough" or "I'll never be able to do this," can erode our self-confidence and limit our potential. In contrast, positive self-talk can boost our self-esteem, increase our motivation, and improve our mental health. In this article, we will explore the benefits of cultivating positive self-talk and offer strategies for improving your inner dialogue.

What is Positive Self-Talk?

Positive self-talk is the practice of using optimistic, encouraging, and empowering language when talking to ourselves. It involves replacing negative or self-critical thoughts with positive affirmations that promote self-love, self-acceptance, and self-growth. Positive self-talk can help us reframe challenging situations, overcome obstacles, and cultivate a sense of resilience and confidence.

Benefits of Positive Self-Talk

Cultivating positive self-talk has numerous benefits, including:

Improved mood: Positive self-talk can help us shift our focus from negative thoughts tò more optimistic and hopeful ones, improving our mood and reducing stress and anxiety.

Increased self-esteem: Positive self-talk can help us develop a more positive self-image, increasing our confidence and self-esteem.

Enhanced performance: Positive self-talk can help us stay motivated and focused, improving our performance in academic, personal, or professional endeavors.

Improved relationships: Positive self-talk can help us develop healthier relationships with ourselves and others, leading to more positive interactions and greater satisfaction in our social lives.

Strategies for Cultivating Positive Self-Talk

Here are some strategies for cultivating positive self-talk:

Identify your negative self-talk patterns: The first step in cultivating positive self-talk is to become aware of your negative thought patterns. Pay attention to your inner dialogue and notice when you're being self-critical or pessimistic.

Reframe negative thoughts: Once you've identified your negative self-talk patterns, reframe them into more positive and empowering statements. For example, if you catch yourself thinking, "I'm not good enough," replace it with, "I am capable and worthy."

Use affirmations: Affirmations are positive statements that you repeat to yourself to reinforce positive beliefs and self-talk. Examples of affirmations include "I am worthy of love and respect," "I am capable of achieving my goals," and "I trust in my abilities and decisions."

Practice gratitude: Gratitude is a powerful tool for cultivating positive self-talk. Focus on what you are grateful for in your life, and use these positive feelings to counteract negative self-talk.

Surround yourself with positive influences: Surround yourself with positive people, books, podcasts, and other resources that reinforce positive self-talk and help you maintain a positive mindset.

Celebrate your achievements: Celebrate your successes, no matter how small. Acknowledge your hard work and achievements, and use these positive feelings to reinforce your self-talk.

Conclusion

Cultivating positive self-talk is a powerful way to improve your mood, increase your self-esteem, and enhance your performance in all areas of life. By becoming aware of your negative self-talk patterns, reframing negative thoughts into positive affirmations, and surrounding yourself with positive influences, you can improve your inner dialogue and achieve greater happiness and success. Remember to be patient with yourself and practice self-compassion as you work towards cultivating positive self-talk.

Many scientists and researchers have studied the concept of mastering the mind and have found that it is a key factor in achieving success and happiness. Studies have shown that practicing mindfulness, developing positive thinking patterns, and setting goals can lead to improved mental health, increased productivity, and greater well-being.

For example, a 2015 study published in the journal "Mindfulness" found that mindfulness meditation can improve cognitive flexibility and reduce negative thinking patterns. Another study from 2017 published in the "Journal of Happiness Studies" found that setting goals and pursuing them can lead to greater happiness and life satisfaction.

Neuroscience research has also shown that our brains are capable of changing and adapting throughout our lives, and that we can rewire our brains to develop more positive thinking patterns. This concept is known as neuroplasticity and has been studied extensively in recent years.

In summary, scientists have found that mastering your mind involves a combination of strategies such as mindfulness, positive thinking, goal setting, and neuroplasticity. By practicing these strategies regularly, we can improve our mental health and well-being, and achieve greater success and happiness in life.

"The mind is everything. What you think, you become." - Buddha

"The mind is not a vessel to be filled, but a fire to be kindled." - Plutarch

"The mind is like a parachute, it works best when it's open." - Frank Zappa

"The mind is not a thing, it is a process... It is not a computing machine, it is a dance." - Francisco Varela

"The human mind is not a static entity. It evolves and changes, and with that evolution and change, problems and challenges arise." - Albert Bandura

www.ingramcontent.com/pod-product-compliance
Lightning Source LLC
LaVergne TN
LVHW090334210926
848480LV00004B/1403